The *Faces* OF ASCENSION

·················

BOOK 15

VERLING CHAKO PRIEST, Ph.D

Order this book online at www.trafford.com
or email orders@trafford.com

Most Trafford titles are also available at major online book retailers.

Print information available on the last page.

ISBN: 978-1-4907-8112-9 (sc)
ISBN: 978-1-4907-8113-6 (hc)
ISBN: 978-1-4907-8114-3 (e)

Library of Congress Control Number: 2017902556

Trafford rev. 02/21/2017

www.trafford.com
North America & international
toll-free: 1 888 232 4444 (USA & Canada)
fax: 812 355 4082

Contents

Contents

ACKNOWLEDGMENTS

I wish to thank all of the Masters, God, and Gaia for giving of their precious time to write a chapter/epic for my/Jeshua's book on *Ascension*. I certainly could not have done this without them, for I, too, had some confusion as to the meaning of Ascension. I think the many *faces* they presented offered the readers and me a working paradigm for a better understanding of Ascension.

Heather Clarke is my editor, and she kept her professional eye on my many commas, or lack thereof. Thank you so much, dear friend.

I thank all of you readers for your loyalty and love you send to me with each purchase of my books. It has been my endeavor to provide you with new ideas and thoughts so that you could change any outdated belief systems that are misleading you on your path.

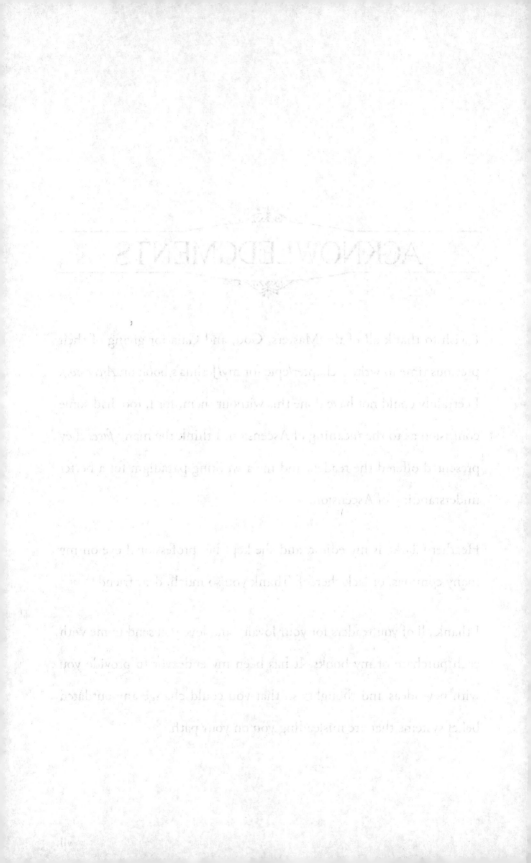

DEDICATION

I dedicate Book 15 to those Entities who are striving so

sincerely and diligently toward their Ascension. May

God bless them as they journey back to Him.

FOREWORD

I had finished my last book almost a year ago. In fact, I had written two books in 2015—*TRANSITIONS* and a sequel *TRANSITIONS Vol. II*. I felt elated and somewhat drained at the same time. When I thought of writing another book in 2016, I drew a blank. I had absolutely no idea for a new book. So I just let it rest. You have heard about that saying, *let go; let God*. That is what I did.

A few months went by during which I had what I call *coughing fits*. After my daughter visited me over Thanksgiving, she urged me to see a doctor. I had the usual tests—lung X-ray (normal); blood white-cell count (normal, showing no infection). However, one other blood test showed a high allergy condition. But to what??

The only new holistic supplement I had taken for the last few months was one made of various seeds. I immediately cancelled my monthly order and threw away what seeds I had on hand. There was almost an immediate relief from my coughing bouts upon cessation of this supplement.

Meanwhile, I had received during a reading that my next book would be on *Ascension—The Truth of Ascension*, she told me. (I wish to keep the Reader anonymous.) I was excited to get started. Jeshua came forth and verified that I would indeed be writing on *Ascension*. However, what with my cough allergy and the holidays the start of my book was slow going. (My launch date: 09-22-16)

Nevertheless, I did persevere and brought in wonderful teachings from many Masters—which you are about to read. I will talk with you again in the Epilogue. Enjoy!

INTRODUCTION

09-22-16 5:05 AM *Good morning, precious one. We are off on the start of our wonderful new book:* The Truth of Ascension. *And yes, 'tis I; I am Sananda of the Christ Consciousness. This book is much needed, for it is coming to the point when much of humanity will be making its Ascension. No one is left behind. The Ascension, you see, is by choice. There is always a choice in whatever you do—in little miniscule things as a child throwing snow balls at a passerby or as an adult making the commitment to ascend.*

Ascension has many faces. People think it just happens and they can't particularly think of anything they have done towards it. But you see, all of their life they have been moving to that grand finale. Most people sleep through their lifetime. And I do not mean their physical sleep when their head is on a pillow. I mean they are not awake spiritually. They go about their daily business—their tasks. Some love; some cheat. Some give; some hoard and are stingy. Some have a conscious idea of what they are doing, while others are doing what can be called *unconscious acts.*

Now we are writing this book—and I say *we* because there will be many Masters coming through, which for unbelievers is always a little disconcerting. Whether to believe the material or not is still your choice. Are you able to hear the truth? Are you awake?

There are many dimensions to an Ascension. The majority of humanity has been in what is termed third dimension—3D. That is where the motto seemed to be—get anything free and just for me, as in *me, myself* and *I.* Then humanity moved up and is now mostly in the 4th dimension, 4D, although there are always the stragglers—always the last to grow, to evolve, to expand; always the last to seek their own salvation, shall we say; always the last to act in a positive, conscious way.

Conscious people are kind. They are giving; they are aware of other people and have much self-awareness. They may be taking selfies with their smart phones, but they are still self-aware and are thinking whom to give to. It may surprise you to learn that this author does not own a smart phone. She still has the small flip-top one she uses on occasion. She has not joined social media where she would have become involved in discussions or retorts to others. She did not want to be inundated with e-mails every time she wrote a remark and to have to defend her statements. She is what one could call a *senior-senior*. She has learned much throughout her long lifetime and is very wise.

Her channeling ability has developed so that she is able to telepathically tap into what the Masters are saying to her and for her ears alone at times. And yes, we still have to lower our energy to meet her, but that is not a bad thing. We lower so we do not burn her body up. At the same time, she raises her vibrations in order to meet us half way.

Now is not everything I have been saying a discussion of Ascension? Ascension is everyday living—living to your utmost, always aware of your neighbors or brothers or sisters, never alone, never. For those of you who are not quite sure what I am talking about, I have said that Ascension has many dimensions. You can be like this channel, sitting in the alcove of her bedroom where she channels her many books. The room is silent because of the early morning hours. There is no one in the house but her. And yet she is not alone. Arch Angel Michael has put many angels around her.

Saint Germaine has his Violet Flame encasing her.

Mother Mary has her soft, loving colors wafting over her.

And I am Jeshua/Jesus/Sananda of the Christ Consciousness, speaking to her through the recording device. So if a person walked into the room and observed what was going on, he or she would be amazed at the activity of the other dimensions.

There has been much reported about the symptoms of Ascension. Some have periods of feeling dizzy or light headed, and others just feel they want to take a nap. Still others have a certain name or phrase they wish to express and when they try to say it, the word is gone. They have to ask their angels, *what was that word I wanted*? And then it comes to them. They have aches and pain throughout their body— God's gift of His energies. It makes people tired and they ache. Of course the trick is to be able to differentiate those symptoms from a medical issue that needs attention.

Some people never go to a doctor. But that is not a particular training. It is merely the DNA structure of their body. It can tolerate strong energies. Or as the saying goes, *it just never gets sick*. Some of the readers may be saying, *why can't I be like that?* Well, when you were drawing up your contract for this lifetime, you chose the body that you have. That DNA may have many aches and pains with many trips to the doctor for this and that.

So you see, it does not mean one person is better than another simply because he or she does not see a doctor. It simply means the DNA of that body is different from yours. However, the good news is when you have ascended, you will no longer need medical help in any way or form. You will be in a higher dimension.

This channel is very careful about plagiarism, so she is censoring the statement that I was going to repeat that we had heard from someone else the other evening. But I can say that you will have no more aches and pains after you ascend.

Humanity is quite fearful of what is known as the Unidentified Flying Objects (UFOs). Humanity is also ignorant of the fact that these flying machines carry Ambassadors from other Universes. They carry Masters. I have my own ship—*The New Jerusalem*—with the Galactic Federation Commander Ashtar. Many of you have your own ships, and yes, they will be smaller, but they are still a ship.

There are millions of ships surrounding this planet, in and out, under the seas, inside the planet, over the skies. They are everywhere and they have the ability to be what is referred to as *cloaked*. It is like a fog; you cannot see through it, but there is a ship through the fog. When the time comes that the fog lifts— it is called *the Disclosure*—you then will see the ships, and it will be announced that they are here.

Many of the ships are healing ships. You are taken aboard and healed. Your old age and infirmaries will disappear. You will walk off the ship with the vim and vigor of youth once again, looking as you did around the age of 30.

What has this got to do with Ascension, you may be asking? It is all part of Ascension. It is joy. Many people think, *how can I be joyful when I have a decrepit old body that I no longer can think in, act in, or eat in?* Therefore, you are given a young body so you can continue your progression to higher consciousness in greater comfort, clarity, and in joy.

This is an *Introduction* to this book. It is not meant to be academic, for you could be bored when you turned the pages. This book is to bring you joy and excitement as you turn each page to read what the next wonderment will be on your journey.

Your soul is magnificent and vibrant, and it needs a vibrant body. You can take your body with you now as you ascend. That was written up in the Bible when I did it thousands of years ago. Remember I told you that all of you would be able to do what I was doing. I did nothing that you would not be able to do if you wished. I was in a human body. I ascended with my body just as you will IF you wish. Some people may not want to ascend with their body. They just want to leave it behind. Again it is all a matter of choice.

Dear ones, I have given you little tidbits to think about. But I want you to think about the joy you will be in. You will no longer—using the terms *sweat* and *slave*—over your jobs. You will be doing things you have a passion for, a love for, as that brings you much happiness.

This planet will no longer have wars, conflicts. It is a beautiful planet with wonderful vegetation, a large variety of colorful animals that will eat only fruits, nuts and vegetables. You will no longer eat meats; as Zorra, the son of Prime Creator says, *eat nothing with faces*. Therefore, animals will no longer feel threatened by you and their heads will not hang from your walls. You will no longer be proud of your tiger rugs. The fur coats are no longer used to impress but in the frigid north they are used for warmth, not always with the consent of the animal. But, you see, there will no longer be those icy places. The temperatures will be moderate—around 75 degrees Fahrenheit or so. The planet you see is ascending also right along with you.

I am going to step back now for another Master will be coming forth with his segment.

I bless all the readers of this book. Hold it to your heart and feel my love for you. I am your brother, Sananda.

Oh, thank you, Lord. You are most welcome, our dearest channel. I know typing this up may be a little more difficult for you because of the strength of your eyesight. But that too shall pass. That too will be healed.

Until we meet again, dear one; much love to you.

Thank you Lord; love you back. Namaste.

Namaste.

1

SAINT GERMAINE

09-24-16 Saturday 5:05 AM.

Good morning, precious one; all up and ready, we see. This morning we start the book in earnest. I gave you the book's Introduction *on Thursday; you transcribed it Friday and then sent it off to our editor, Heather Clarke. Now here it is Saturday, and you are raring to go. There are many Angels around you. AA Michael has cleared your space. The Master who will be speaking is standing by, so I will step back now.* Thank you, Jeshua.

Good morning, my precious sister; I am Saint Germaine. *Oh, Saint Germaine, hello.* Hello, my dear one. Remember I told you a few years ago that you, Jeshua and I rode a tandem bike together. You steered the handle bars and I, Saint Germaine, rode in the middle.

And now here I am back once again to give you your first chapter for this wonderful book on Ascension. I am honored, and I thank you for receiving me. *Oh Saint Germaine, it is with very little effort on my part to receive you, I assure you (chuckles)!*

The Lightworkers of humanity have Ascension foremost on their minds. They are very aware of the importance of what they are doing; what they are thinking; what they are reading; what they are listening to, for they know that every act influences their progression of Ascension.

Readers, you have heard, I am sure, to moderate and to turn off the TV if it is violent, for anything negative will influence your own vibrations. Of course in America the focus is on the political scene. Since the election is in November, the negative jabs the two candidates give to each other is revving up. I will say no more, for the scene must play itself out. It will have a grand finale that one no-one will be expecting. Just know that the God of this planet and Prime Creator of this world are watching. And the Galactics are watching also.

I must add one more thing. People worry about being attacked by nuclear weapons. There will be no nuclear conflagrations. Relax, people. Whoever pushes the red button will find that it malfunctions.

Nothing will work, thanks to our brothers and sisters in the skies. Release your fears.

Now back to the book on *Ascension*. Lightworkers carry a great deal of Light and have high vibrations. They are very much aware that every act and thought influences their progression. There are different forms of Ascension, as you must know by now. The one most people know of is written in the Bible, telling of Jesus ascending with his body. The earth just fell away from his feet. Up he went with a swift whoosh, and he was gone.

Other forms of Ascension, of course, are when the body dies. The soul leaves and goes to the higher realms which you call *Heaven* or *Nirvana*. He or she has ascended. Even the person you think of as a sinner ascends when he or she transitions. Then let the lessons begin. He has his life's review and finds out his actions were not the kind to make him proud.

People with addictions have a difficult time moving forward because they are so stuck in that lifetime. I will use the example of *alcoholics*. Their body craves that liquor. In order to satisfy the pain of **not** having a drink, they gulp it and then have the pain of being drunk. At that moment there is no ascension. It is a stalemate—no progression.

They sober up and then after a few hours the craving starts again and intensifies until they ingest the liquor which starts the cycle all over again. Then when their body dies and the soul travels to where it is guided to go, and they review that lifetime, they question why they could not have stopped this addiction. So the lessons begin all over again. (*It will take several lifetimes to break this cycle.*)

They take another lifetime to try to overcome that addiction, for they will be addicted again, you see, to whatever stopped them the first time—be it heavy drugs, alcohol, and even the craving for food. When their body has become over 600 pounds, it cannot move; it just vegetates in bed and craves to eat. The fatter they become, the larger the appetites—addictions to food. And yes, it is psychological, and they hate themselves and are in pain. One cannot help but have compassion for them.

Then the body dies and the soul is ejected to Heaven and has its review. The soul begs not to return to Earth; not to return to a body. But the soul must descend in order to turn the situation around—to not be addicted to food again; to not be addicted to alcohol again. I could go on repeatedly about the different addictions people get themselves into. You must know by now it is psychological in nature. The soul is fighting for its ascension—or one could say it is fighting for its life.

After a soul is ejected from its body, it has more awareness because it can read the Akashic records. And I really do not need to tell you that a soul does not ascend with a 600 pound body. So Ascension, as Sananda was saying, has many faces.

Now, let us say the soul is in Heaven. Can it ascend in Heaven? Of course it can. No one is never not moving either up or down. He is constantly moving with his choices. If the soul wishes to reincarnate, he goes down. If the soul is advanced enough to join its soul group, it ascends even more. In the soul group, the soul's awareness strengthens, advances, evolves, expands, and the soul ascends upward. Ascension has so many dimensions, it is difficult to put a mathematical number on them.

God is still ascending. Your planet is still ascending. You know, when a planet evolves and expands and has all these creatures—human and animal—on it, it becomes very difficult to ascend.

Have you seen a dog nursing her puppies? All of a sudden she stands up and all the puppies slide off her. Now think of your planet—the Earth. She has all these creatures, these puppies, sucking off her. She wants to stand up and climb higher. But every time she moves, her puppies come tumbling down—(*a metaphor for earthquakes*). It becomes quite a dilemma for her.

She realizes that humanity must evolve also, as she would no longer be able to fulfill its needs. She will not be held back, however. A mother creature must go find sustenance for herself. Anything clinging to her will fall to the wayside. It is not done with anger and meanness. It is done because the mother also needs to expand—ascend. So there is another face of Ascension.

Her oceans have been polluted. She must cleanse herself. Her rivers and streams are polluted, many from the run-off of factories. Oil drilling injures her. The mother is hurting because her arteries are plugged, just like a human's. Her heart is in pain also like a human with the wars and many conflicts, the killings. Therefore, you see that Ascension is imperative for your planet or **she** will die. People killing people on her does not help with her own vibration. It brings her down. She cannot turn off the TV and go take a walk in Nature. She can only rise and shake a bit to lessen the tension so that she may keep on ascending, not become stagnant and find herself sinking.

Dear friends, I have brought you a way of looking at Ascension. It is a wonderful progression of the soul. Let go of all the Biblical terms and references and seek the truth of it. Look at all of your activities. Are you ascending? Or are you walking to the nearest bar? Or are you in bed waiting for your next meal? Always, dear friends, *ask what am I doing; what am I thinking; is it helping me make my ascension?* If you cannot get a strong *YES*, then change your attitude; change something you are doing; change something within you. A human response many times *can* be: *there's nothing wrong with me; why should I change?* That statement alone tells you that you have just condemned yourself. Do not be afraid of change, dear friends. It is a good thing!

I leave you now. I watch over you. Many of you use my Violet Flame that I have given to humanity. It will help you make many changes— the good kind for your body. I cover you with my Violet Flame and my love.

I AM Saint Germaine.

Thank you Lord. That was different and wonderful, and I thank you for it.

You are most welcome, my dear sister, and I leave you with my love.

2

MOTHER MARY

09-29-16 Thursday 5:08 – 5:55 AM; Chapter 2.

Good morning, precious one. All set to start Chapter 2, we see. I will be bringing forth a Lady Master who will give you the next chapter on Ascension. I will step aside now.

Oh, good morning, my precious child. I am Mother Mary. *Oh, hello, Mother Mary.* It has been a long time since we last spoke like this, although we converse frequently in the upper spheres. Now this is Chapter 2, and this is my segment. I will follow the leader here, and we will talk about the Ascension and give you another face of it.

As a baby, we are born pure and perfect. Most parents love their baby child, while some parents do not want it. Other parents who may be single with no means of supporting the child may give it up for adoption. But this baby is still perfect.

At the moment the little one takes a breath, he or she starts on the road to Ascension. (*I will just make the pronouns singular at this point.*) Her soul has not entered the wee body yet, but it is very close. The strength of this energy, you see, could be damaging to this fragile form. So the soul will enter the small child around the age of 6-7. In the meantime, her soul stays close and monitors everything that happens to the tiny babe until it is strong enough to accommodate the soul's energy.

As the child matures, she will start that long road in education—school days that make many a parent groan, I *don't know how to do that new math!* The child struggles too, because she is not used to being around such a mass of students. However, pretty soon, she settles down into the way of school life.

School can be a deterrent to Ascension. When one thinks, *well, if school turns out to be a horrible experience, I have wasted a lot of time that could have been focused on Ascension.* But that is not true. Even the worst experiences of other kids being mean, or stealing your lunch money, or other things that can make a person unhappy are experiences the soul has chosen. It is called *honing.* It is honing itself—growing a second skin, so to speak. While it is a struggle, all of that is also advancement on the road to Ascension.

Now if the person, we will say our little school girl, turns to her shadow side and turns mean and revengeful and starts playing the dark games that are being played on her, she is not progressing. It becomes two steps forward and three steps back. Therefore, those twelve years of school, one could say, is a *make-or-break* experience.

The soul is gaining the experience it wants, but it may not be to the advantage it was hoping for. So you see, readers, your school years are very important for Ascension. The student then has a choice whether to go on to college for higher learning or to enter the work place right after high school. All of that then becomes a different game, does it not? College offers difficult situations in learning while preparing the person for life amongst humanity.

Now let us fast forward a bit and say that the schoolgirl has graduated. All formal school education has been completed, and she is in the work force of young people. She is in the age group of around twenty, most likely. The next ten years will try her in a way that she never expected, for you see, now she has the struggle of a maturing body. There are decisions to make about her body. One of the biggest decisions is how far is she going to go when in love. Does she follow her body's desires and have sexual relationships and if she becomes pregnant, will she keep the baby or abort it? All of these variables start rearing their head.

It would be interesting if a young person could go through the dimensions, read the Akashic records and see what the game plan is. Is she supposed to get married then? Is she supposed to have a baby? Will she have an early death or a long life? All of this would be very helpful for decision making. The soul rules that area and wants those experiences. If the person has a great deal of awareness and is connected to her soul, she will follow its guidance, and her progression with Ascension will be swift. However, how many people are consciously connected to their soul? Not too many of them, I sadly state.

Therefore, they are being led by their peers. They are being led by the personality of the body—the ego. If they are not that aware, the Ascension could be slow moving up but swift in the downward spiral. Then the person has to start again. As I have said, three steps forward and four or five steps backwards.

Now we have brought our subject, the young girl, to the work place. She has found the man she is supposed to marry—which is all part of the contract, by the way. She has her children, and there are different experiences the soul has set up that she will go through. It depends upon her vocation as to what the adventure will be. Many decisions will be required if she is connected to her soul. The decisions will be swift and the progression will be upward. If she has still not connected with her soul on an awareness level, her decisions could make her slip again—two steps forward; three steps backwards.

Now she is in middle age. She is going through the many experiences with her children that she had—going to school for the first time; handling the dreaded homework. But here, you see, is where the marriage can get a little rocky. The husband and wife have been married several years and have found that there are areas of the marriage that need adjusting and correcting. Addictions could be a big part on adjusting the partnership. Some get divorced; some see it through. Again it is all what was in the contract. *Am I to divorce my partner or am I to tough it through?* Each decision will have its own consequences. Each decision may be correct for that person or may not be.

When I hear clergy telling their congregation about the damnation of divorce, it saddens me. I do not judge, but it saddens me, for clergy hold a great deal of power over their congregation and they are putting out there what is not true, although they believe it. Divorce is an individual decision. Maybe they are meant to stay together, but also maybe they are meant to divorce!

There is nothing sinful in a divorce. I hope you readers take that to heart. Those churches that preach no divorce, that it is a sin, are not speaking the truth. God, I assure you, does not judge a person for having divorced. It could very well have been part of his or her contract. So people, if you are judging your neighbor for having divorced, please let that go. It is whatever the soul has written in that contract. What does the soul want to experience? A divorce can be a progression of Ascension just as staying married can. There are reasons for all decisions.

So we have our young couple, and they are now middle aged and are struggling with each other's idiosyncrasies. They pick out different practices that, shall we say, *bug* them. The husband tells his wife that he hates it when she washes her hands and cleans each fingernail at the same time. The wife retorts that it is better than blowing her nose in her hands when she washes her face! So they retort back and forth naming acts the other one does that triggers a negative response. And if the couple is struggling with addictions, which hold you back from Ascension, the marriage can become quite rocky, as I have said.

Let us continue with our couple. Their children have grown now and the parents are in their retirement years. Are they enjoying those years or are they in fear because they do not have enough money? That seems to be the biggest fear for most people.

If they have saved enough money, do they actually start to travel? Or does the body have so many ailments which prevent them from straying too far from their doctors and what their health insurance will allow. Progression for Ascension can then slow down. One would think that the older one was the swifter Ascension would be. But it seems as if the older the person gets after retirement age, the slower the progression can be. There is always the other side of the coin where the person turns toward spiritual awakenings and his progression becomes quite swift.

The body dies and the soul transitions to the upper spheres. He has a review of his lifetime and sees what he could have done differently. He is the only one judging what he views as his mistakes. He speaks with the Masters who are guiding him and finds that he actually has progressed toward his Ascension and now is ready for the next round—reincarnation.

Therefore, dear readers, you see that your whole life is one of progression forward to Ascension, or a slide downward. It is not a given. You have to strive for it. It is just like when you were in school and you had to strive forward in order to be promoted to the next class and onward to your degrees. Ascension, you could say, is of the highest degree, for now you are speaking of soul work.

I AM Mother Mary, and it has been my greatest pleasure to give you another aspect, another face of Ascension. No one has told you it would be easy, but it is attainable and an attainment that is dearly sought after. It is one of the greatest achievements that a soul can make.

I bless you, dear readers. Namaste!

Thank you, Mother Mary. That was a different way of looking at Ascension and an interesting viewpoint. Everyone's lifetime is a face of Ascension. Thank you.

You are most welcome, dearest one. Adieu.

Adieu.

All right, dear one that was Chapter 2. Much food for thought, which is the object of this book—to give the readers different perspectives on their Ascension. Until next time, dear one. I am Jeshua, with love.

3

GUATAMA BUDDHA

10-07-2016 Friday 5:15 AM – 6:10 AM

Good morning, precious one; here we are all ready to start Chapter 3. This chapter will be a little different for you, but one that gives another face of Ascension.

Good morning, my dear channel. I am known as Buddha. You have talked with me through other channels. I am here to give you another face, another outlook on Ascension. In my day, as I sought to enlighten myself and as the story goes, I sat under the Bodhi tree until I could see the world as it was.

I came from a palace where everything was given to me and then went out among the masses to seek what it was like on the outside. So I sat under this shade tree and watched the poor struggle and watched the rich refuse to give to them. I did not realize as I sat there for many days that I was actually becoming enlightened, I was making an Ascension, you see, just as all of you are.

As I climbed up that ladder of wisdom, I could see clearly where the human beings were getting caught up in all of the physicality of human living. I could see how it was for them—to not think of anything else but survival. Many had just sought a safe place for the night which would be under another tree. The air was warm. It was not the rainy season, so people just laid down more or less where they were to rest a while.

The story goes that I just sat under that Bodhi tree, but that is not entirely true. I did get up and wander around; I asked people questions. I asked what they thought went on behind the palace walls. I got an unadulterated answer, I assure you. The people were ignorant; so many times they were just telling what they had heard. It was gossip. Some tidbits were true; other bits were not.

As I walked among them and begged for my food along with everyone else, eating only what I could that would not take from my neighbor, I gradually laid out the plan that is known as the Eightfold Path or the eight steps to Enlightenment.* In some ways, these steps can be held at the level that you readers are seeking now to ascend, for Ascension is striving for Enlightenment.

As I sat under my Bo tree or walked among the masses, I found that finding a crust of bread or picking a berry could bring me great joy. I found that I was laughing and joking. After I passed by and had had my conversation with the people, they too were smiling as I left them. I thought, *would it not be wonderful if all people could just come from the joy that is in their heart?* I held the babies who were in a more pure state in their hearts. They had not been stained by humanity yet. They smiled and gurgled, held out their arms for me. Is it not so that those who are striving for Ascension hold out their arms for help, as the Ascension symptoms can overpower them at times? At other times they are laughing in joy, similar to how I responded.

I listened to people, for as I listened, I could feel what they were saying. I could feel the emotions. As you readers are in the process of ascending, do you not feel the emotions behind the words that are being said? Let us take the example of politicians, for the election of a new president in America is looming its head in November. Do you not feel what the two candidates are saying? Of course, you realize much of what you are feeling is your own projections onto them. Are you feeling truth? It may be for you, but are you feeling truth from them? Both candidates are struggling with their private demons—keeping them at bay.

In my day when I roamed the streets, people did not recognize me. I looked like all the others. My clothes were slovenly. I bathed when I could but not too often, but I felt such joy that my whole demeanor started to shine. I noticed that people were following me. If I sat down to rest, they sat down and immediately started gossiping back and forth. It was similar to your neighbors coming together and talking about the different aspects of their life. Then if I got up, they got up (*chuckles*). Pretty soon I had a tail of people—I was the puppy dog and the people were the tail, wagging away.

They started asking questions: *what do you do when you are hungry and ask for food and people turn away in disgust?* They yell at you: *why don't you get a job*, not realizing there were no jobs for one of that low caste. And if she were a woman, she would not be that verbal. In my day, women were supposed to be at home taking care of the children, cooking the meals, waiting on the man as he expected and she was expected to obey. That is still the rule, is it not, in some countries even today in 2016?

As you look around and study the faces of your neighbors, everyone is striving to go forward—to go forward with their vocation or to their job. They are walking fast. If it is raining, they are running. In the cities they are stopped at the corners of busy streets with stoplights or policemen. Cars could run them down. In my day, it would be the donkeys and the carts with people sing-song-ing their wares.

They carried everything, for the person who was lucky enough to have a house needed everything daily! *Cabbages for sale; apples for sale; nuts for sale!* The people streamed out with sacks or pails to put the food into. They then carried the food back into the house. Of course, it was always the cooks or houseboys who ran out to buy the goods that were being offered. There was haggling over the price—always haggling. Nothing was taken at face value. If you put that into perspective for this century, would it not seem overwhelming to have each person who wanted to buy something haggling over the price? Is it not easier to have a stated price? People have a choice then to either buy it or not buy it. The noisy haggling just was a way of life.

I then would seek out my Bodhi tree again just to get some peace. I would go inside of me. I had a way where I could just shut out the world. I felt safe, for it was safer for me to just go inside into the private room I had in me. I just shut out the world. I thought and thought of peace and kindness and joy and happiness. I wondered why people could not find that happiness in their heart. I would ponder on this.

Then I would hear my stomach growling, telling me I needed to get up and find something to eat. So I stood up, grabbed my begging bowl and off I would go. The monks who strove by seemed to know what house they could go to for a crust of bread. Some of the houses had very good cooks, and they knew how to make tasty gravy from different vegetables. It was always a great day of rejoicing when you had a full bowl of hot steaming vegetables with gravy and a nice chunk of fresh bread. That brought joy to everyone, and they would talk in an animated way—laugh and smile and eat the last tidbit, wiping their bowl clean with their bread. Then with full bellies, they sat down to rest. They started talking philosophically. Keep in mind, readers, during the time I was seeking my own enlightenment, I was a *nobody*, to use that term. Of course, each person is a precious *somebody* that the Creator knows. But we did not know that yet. We were striving for that—reaching for that—that face of Ascension.

So we sat there and told about our trials and tribulations. I did not speak about my days behind the walls, the palace grounds, and the plentiful food on the tables. When it was not all eaten, it was taken back to the kitchens for the help to eat. There was a back entrance where the poor could come and obtain food. However, the food was given sporadically; it was not hourly. It was similar to farmers throwing the slops out to the pigs. It was the same type of energy—throwing the slops out to humanity.

Readers, as you seek your Ascension, always be aware: *are you in your heart? Are you in joy?* Or *are you throwing the slops out to the masses?* When people enter the bars and become inebriated, are they not throwing their slops out to others? What you carry inside of you and when you give forth your words of wisdom, is it not like handing people loaves of fresh bread? Are not these words food for them? Your words, dear hearts, are food for the thoughts of others. Always think of your words bringing a fullness that maybe others are feeling and seeking. Do not let it be like in antiquity where the slops are thrown out of the window or the door. Your mouth is **your** doorway. Are those words coming out as slops or fresh food? Are they given with joy and peace, or are they given with venom and anger? *You are stupid; what do you know about it?*

So much of what we speak that comes out of the doorway of our mouths can be a cleansing. When we were children, and our parents were not as giving and enlightened as we hoped they would be, or our brothers and sisters, or peers at school, we took upon us their slops, did we not? Now as adults what are we giving out? Give out the love that is in your heart.

Everyone carries a seed of love. Give out your love so when you go amidst a group of people, they start coming up to you and hugging you. *I am so glad to see you!* They like your energy, for you are always smiling, laughing, and being truthful with them. Instead of telling them you are just fine, you briefly comment on an aching shoulder, then add how good it is to see them also. All the faces of Ascension, dear ones.

Ascension is a lifetime of striving. Maybe that lifetime is only a few weeks or one of many, many years. The stories about me sitting under that Bodhi tree have been broadened, and the scribes have made it grander than it was. I was learning also. I was taking those steps forward and then slipped back once in a while. I was not perfect and did not just jump up from that tree after sitting there for weeks all enlightened. I did not do that. It was humanly impossible.

I got up to eat and take care of my bodily needs. I spoke with people and I walked. It was similar to your Master Jesus who walked and walked. I walked! How can you know your neighbor if you stay in place the whole time? How can you know the world? You cannot. You can define your world if it is only the sides of your house. But now-a-days, you have vehicles that allow you to travel great distances. That then becomes your world.

As you travel to different countries, that becomes part of your world that you are seeing, visiting, watching, feeling, and learning. You may like it or not; it is a different culture. How flexible are you, or do you just feel uneasy—even frightened at times? Does the food affect your body in a negative way so that you are throwing up? Each culture will have its idiosyncrasies—its own face. Are you acceptable of this or is it in your nature that everyone must think and feel as you do in order to make you comfortable? You go scurrying back to where you came from.

Readers, everyone is ascending in his or her own way, at his or her own pace, forward or backward, accepting or not, dying and going off to Heaven. But now we are all given the chance to just go forward, ascend and take our bodies with us—to just have the Earth disappear beneath our feet and to step through another door **with** our body. We are going to the great healing ships where we step in with our old age and decrepit bones and then step out again, youthful and beautiful. We can once again run and dance. And we will be enlightened. We will remember all that we did through those many lives. Ascension is what I was doing way back then, sitting under the Bodhi tree. I was becoming enlightened. I was stepping upward. I Am Gautama Buddha, sending you much love. *Thank you, Lord.*

*The Eightfold Path: "Correct view; correct attitude; correct speech; correct action; correct livelihood; correct efforts; correct mindfulness; correct meditation". (Circa 6 – 4 century.) Wikipedia Encyclopedia: "About Buddha."

4

KUAN YIN

10-11-16 Tuesday, Chapter 4, 4:45 AM – 5:30 AM.

Good morning, precious one, all set to bring in Chapter 4. Yes. *All right, let's get started. This is going to be a feminine energy to get another viewpoint. I will step aside, as she is waiting, as they all are. As you know, they do line up for our books.* Yes (chuckles), thank you so much.

Good morning, fair lady; I am known as Kuan Yin. *Oh, how nice; I greet you, thank you for coming.* You are welcome; we love doing this. We have done this before for your other books. Today we are to give you a chapter on *Ascension*.

I wish to refer back to ancient China. You have read and I have told you in the past that the Chinese did not honor their girl babies. They used them as sex toys; they bound their feet, which was excruciating for them. When they reached their pre-teen years, the child would become more enticing to the male suitor. And, oh yes, they picked out the young girls and started their sexual favors early on in that sweet girl's life. But that was the way of life then.

However, it stopped the growth of the child—we'll say the spiritual growth of the child. She was forced to think of little but her physical sufferings. Obviously that would not enhance any Ascension. But I need to back up a little, for you know now, readers, when you go through periods such as trials and tribulations that are forced upon you, it has a growth for that soul. It brings a person great wisdom. She learns deeply and can read the emotions of the men. She becomes very wise. (*This is similar to being "street-wise," only it is "men-wise."*) So in this you see there is a growth for Ascension.

Then, which situation becomes the stronger—the one where she knows men or the one where she becomes weaker and gives over her autonomy? We women in the Heavenlies gave great rejoicing when women's feet were finally allowed to grow. We are speaking of history, advancement, and culture, are we not? It seems that if someone waits long enough, there will be a change in one direction or another. And we in the Heavenlies rejoiced when the direction to stop mutilating the bodies of the female children took effect.

As the women matured, they still had that mentality of pleasing the man. Therefore, they would be in their shadow side when another girl received more attention than they did. I see this even to this century where women become jealous of perhaps their sisters, or if their boyfriends look at another girl. Jealousy is one of the features of the shadow side.

Also in Chinese history, when the dictators dictated what people could wear, everyone wore that blue clothing and they all looked the same. The women were not allowed to have beautiful clothes.

The Chinese are exquisite in creating beautiful artifacts.

The embroidery was so lovely also; they used real jewels—pearls, sapphires, rubies, emeralds, and even diamonds if they were that prosperous. Of course, there were the guards guarding the woman if she left the gates of her palatial residence in her finery. The blue uniform that was required later squelched any creativity that the women would like to have shown. So there were these dark periods in Chinese history. I would call them *growing pains,* and each country seems to have them.

These growing pains also created an opportunity where people could shake off the strict fetters of the governments and bring forth new ideas which frequently entailed bloody wars—civil wars among people. But then civilizations and cultures of the people would advance and another era would begin.

It then becomes plain to see that the face of Ascension had many fits and starts—painful starts, painful fits, before culture would settle down and the masses could get in touch with their creativity once again.

Lest you think that the Chinese were in their dark creations entirely, I wish to negate that, for they had loving natures that did come out in their families. The mothers, on the whole, loved their children. Yes, they did have *Ah-mas*—the second mothers—and in America's history, you had the black *Mammies* who loved the white babies who were given to their care. It was the heart that just loved the babies. To this day it is still so. People just love the babies, no matter what color their skin. They are so sweet and innocent and pure in their thoughts and actions. And ascending. (*I have a new great-granddaughter. At 6 weeks, the 5 verbs that seem to describe her actions are: gurgle, smile, eat, burp, and poop. She is covered in kisses throughout the day!*)

The Chinese are also very intelligent. They would teach people in groups. In antiquity, many could not read or write, but there were people like Confucius who would teach only a sentence or two which the masses could remember and quote to others. *Confucius says…** The people would listen and practice what Confucius had said. That would raise their vibratory rate and ascension.

However, it does seem that adversity is the tool that is used to raise one's consciousness. I wish I could say it is love that dominates in the raising of consciousness, but it seems that souls do want to have and learn from these experiences. They take all the dark scenarios and choose to play them out in a particular lifetime to get the experience. And then they see how they can take that experience and turn it into a positive ascension. I know it seems to be the way to advance, but I wish advancement could come from love versus pain.

In other books of this channel, I came forth and told about some of my adventures. I, too, went through the binding of feet as a child.

Another practice that Chinese did in antiquity was to introduce the juice of the poppy at an early age to the child. When the child was in pain with her bound feet, she was given drops of the poppy which would sooth her and let her sleep. And it would let the Ahma and the rest of the household sleep also.

The physicians were wise, however, and warned the parents and Ahmas, *only one or two drops*, otherwise they would go from one trial to another trial—one of addiction and withdrawal. Nothing like having a heroin addict at the age of five! It depended, of course, on the intelligence of the parents and Ahmas. They would put the juice on their finger and let the infant suck that finger. It was absorbed by the infant, which helped both the young one and the adult, otherwise she would eventually be overdosed if it were not sucked off.

These are all faces of Ascension. I believe, readers, you are getting a picture now that Ascension is everyday living—how you meet the happenings of your day. Can you be in joy; can you be in love? Or are you jealous or headstrong and not listening to people who have acquired more wisdom than you at your particular age?

I am known as the Goddess Kuan Yin, but you see, that is an Ascension name; is it not? You readers are gods and goddesses in your own right, for you have had numerous lifetimes. Your soul has honed itself in this lifetime. This is the one that everyone signed up for— to ascend with the maximum Ascension—for I have said there are steps of Ascension along the way in all your lives. In some lives, the steps were downward as your addictions grabbed hold of you. In other lifetimes, the steps were upward as you found love and were loved.

Nothing is more beautiful than when lovers come together for the first time. They respect each other; they hold each other with an endearing reverence. The little idiosyncrasies that will nag at them a few years later are but a brushing glance. Each partner is held, as I have said, in reverence or put on a pedestal. It is sweet to see the looks they give each other that are filled with love. At that time of their lives, they are advancing. Their vibratory rates are increasing. Each sweet embrace and kiss is expressing the love that they have for each other.

And yet the soul has planned a few trials. There could be accidents in sports. There could be car accidents. There could be life-threatening illnesses. There could be death of their babies. All of these things stretch and stress the love between the partners. Some will snap like a rubber band and they will separate. Others tighten the embrace and weather it through.

So when you start a new life, you do not know what you are getting yourself into. Some request an early death, for they do not like all of the discomforts of old age. They do not like the way an old body looks—muscles sagging, skin no longer elastic. They lose their vitality. Therefore, they chose one of their various windows to pass through.

Others want the challenge of being old. Maybe they had passed early in their previous lifetime, so that in this one, they can see what it is like to be old—really old. Be careful of what you ask for. Be careful!

Dear readers, I have told you about more faces of Ascension. I AM Kuan Yin. I give you my blessings.

Thank you, Lady Kuan Yin; thank you so much for coming.

You are most welcome. Greetings.

All right, dear one; we did it.

Yes, we did (chuckling). Each time I wonder: will I? And then answer myself: yes, I can!

*Confucius says: "To see and listen to the wicked is already the beginning of wickedness."

"Think in terms of a year, plant a seed. Think in terms of ten years, plant a tree. Think in terms of a hundred years, teach the people."

Quotes are from Wikipedia Encyclopedia.

5

MARY MAGDALENE

5:30 – 6:10 AM.

Good morning, my precious one; all set to bring in Chapter 5. I commend you for plugging away. Yes, I am really caught up in it—no backing out now *(chuckles). All right, dear one, we are bringing in another woman. She is one you have channeled many times in the past, so I will step back now and let her come forth.* All right.

Good morning, my dear sister. I am Mary Magdalene. *Oh hello, Mary.* I am to talk about some of the faces of Ascension.

As you are beginning to realize, readers, it is not as simple a task as you may have imagined. You were brought up by your parents. You took on their ideas and perspectives of life; whether it was Truth or not, it was their Truth. They passed their Truth on to you. Now you have that daunting task, or privilege, however you want to look at it, of dissecting and asking yourself, *is this really the Truth? Is the belief system I have been carrying all of these years the Truth, or do I need to change in some ways?* For some, change is not that difficult. Others are so embedded into their beliefs that they have no doubt they are right, so therefore, why change?

Some people believe there are no UFOs and The Galactic Federation of Light does not exist. Other people know that the Lord Ashtar has a magnificent space ship—*The New Jerusalem*—which is 2000 miles long and 1000 miles wide. Now who is going to believe that? Can a ship be so large it cannot land (*chuckles*)? Where would it land? It cannot land on top of buildings—2000 miles! It is beyond most people's comprehension.*

Some people cannot believe there are spiritual Masters they can contact. They have read about them, but the only thing they think may be true is what they read/hear about Jesus. Jesus, the love of my life, has quite a reputation, does he not? And his energy has prevailed over this planet for many an aeon.

So, dear readers, when we talk about faces of Ascension, would not your collection of belief systems be another face? It most certainly is. I am giggling now—how many people do you think can ascend if they believe there is no ascension or they believe there are no Masters? They hardly believe in the Supreme Being, the God of this Universe, or the Luminescents as they are also called—*each creating its own world and Universe.*

If you do not believe there is a spiritual stairway to Ascension, how would you seek it to climb it? You see that belief system becomes a face, does it not?

For centuries, people have debated back and forth about this idea and that idea. Some go to lectures; some go to college for the higher learning. All are seeking answers, whether they know it or not. And what are the predominant questions? Most questions are: *What is my purpose for being here? Who am I? How do I finish up this life?* Some truly think they just drop dead in one way or another—from accidents (*no such thing as accidents*), illnesses, or in their sleep. And that's it. They are put in a hole in the ground; people come and cry that they're gone. But that's it! And life goes on.

In the Wild West of yesteryear, people were quick to settle any argument with a gun. Bang-bang and you were dead. (I believe they even have a song named that—*Bang-bang...**) That was a face of Ascension.

Then ask this question: *Can you ascend if you are constantly killing someone and stepping over him to climb further up?* And then it gets back to *contracts*. What's in his contract? Are you killing what's-his-name because he is a so-called bad guy and you had the opportunity to get rid of him? Or are you killing him because he killed you some lifetimes ago? Contracts are very intricate and very tricky.

The political scene that is looming in America in just a handful of days (11-08-16) may have you wondering: what is the contract? *You will be president.* Or who has the contract that states, *you will be the protagonist?* Or, who has the contract where it is stated, *you will be written in as president?* Would that not be another face of Ascension? And would that not offer a president many opportunities to advance up Jacob's ladder or to slide down it? Again, it gets back to belief systems, does it not? How was that candidate raised? Whose belief system has he/she absorbed? Has that system ever changed? In other words, if you are a person of the world, you must have an intricate belief system monitoring the affairs of the world. Going to country to country, either bringing peace or feathering your own cap, would bring many belief systems, distorted or real.

So, dear readers, we have spent twenty minutes speaking about one of the faces of Ascension. As you ponder some of what I have said to you, it will automatically bring up in your mind your philosophy, your psychology. You see how closely it is all related. You cannot have a belief system without it having some type of psychological foundation.

What is the psychological base of a person who had abusive parents? It certainly would hold fear; it would certainly hold mistrust. It would create your particular perspective of life. Therefore, one of your faces is definitely built on your psychology of life. And sorry to say, much of it goes back to parenting. If a parent was loving and giving to her child, that child would be loving and giving in return.

But then you see the soul gets into the act by wanting to experience the life it is leading. It may want a little excitement to see what that would be like. And yes, the soul could be of a giving, loving nature, but what would it be like to turn ugly and wear what is termed another hat—a *dark hat?* What would that be like when those kinds of adventures came to it? Again, what is the contract? But psychology is definitely one of the faces of Ascension. Now, you may not be thinking in terms of psychology, but that is what it means. It is the fits and starts; it is the make-up of people. Even Buddha sitting under his Bodhi tree had a psychological base. I will not analyze my dear brother, that wonderful, giving man. (I am still talking of Buddha in case you are wondering.) Psychology plays a great role in Ascension.

Have you thought how Ascension plays out for married—we will just say—for couples? Do you think they are ascending together? Or does one climb higher than the other? It depends on how long they have been together and it depends on their psychological base.

Some women climb up that ladder, or you may think of it as a staircase, and may go at it in a faster way than their partner. But then they get tested and blocks start coming up. Maybe they lose children in childbirth. How do they handle diversity? Does it bring the couple closer together, or do they in their grief no longer wish to be with each other? So does not *diversity* become a face of Ascension? How is that grief handled? Have they started to slip down the stairs versus climbing joyfully up? (And you realize there are no stairs or ladders. These are only used as metaphors to help you grasp just what you are doing.) We are talking about *vibrations*. When you are in joy and love and in your heart, your vibration increases and you soar. That is all part of Ascension.

Dear ones, we are coming to the end of my time with you. Ponder what I have said; ponder the different faces I have given you for Ascension. Ascension is real, not some nebulous act you cannot grab hold of. It is real. You could say it is similar to a swing; you either go up or you go down. It all depends upon you—your actions, your belief systems, your psychology.

I leave you now with those thoughts. I hold you in my heart, dear ones. I AM Mary Magdalene.

Oh, thank you so much, Mary. That was an entirely different way of looking at Ascension. Thank you so much!

You are most welcome. We did have fun together back in those far distant times, didn't we—both loving our dear Jesus, which we still do, in our own separate ways. *Yes, we do.* And we are still connected to him in our way. *Yes, I know that.*

Until another time, my dear sister, adieu. *Thank you, Mary.*

All right, dear one, you did it. That was my other half, my twin flame, for you readers who do not know. Each of you has your own twin flame whom you know or will meet at some time. So dear one, you have lots to type up. Enjoy the Election Day (*chuckles*). I Am Jeshua, with love.

*The lights of the *New Jerusalem* was the *star* that led the Wise Men to Baby Jesus.

**Bang-Bang* was a popular song that was sung several years ago. You can listen to it sung by various singers through YouTube. I liked

Nancy Sinatra's rendition. I have copied some of the lyrics below. Go to YouTube for the remaining lyrics.

I was 5 and he was 6.

We rode on horses made of sticks.

He wore black and I wore white.

He would always win the fight.

Bang-bang, he shot me down.

Bang-bang I hit the ground.

Bang-bang, that awful sound.

Bang-bang, my baby shot me down.

It has a catching tune. People were singing it all over the country.

6

ASHTAR & DJWAL KHUL

5:20 – 6:20 AM, November 11, 2016

Good morning, precious one; up bright and early I see. Yes. *And this will be Chapter 6 coming up. I will step aside now. He is waiting in the wings, and you will have a delightful time.* All right; thank you *(chuckles)*.

Hello, my dear one. *Hello, Lord; I do not know who you are yet.* Why, I am Ashtar *(chuckles)*. You have been asking for me and now I am here! *Thank you, Ashtar.* I am delighted, my dear sister, to speak with you once again. It has been a long time, has it not? *Yes, and Lord Ashtar, I am so appreciative of your coming this morning.* It will be a delightful time for me to speak on Ascension.

I have seen so many people come to Ascension. They are somewhat beaten up. They have had a hard time climbing Jacob's ladder. I want to gather them into my arms and say, *but dear souls, it need not have been that difficult. You made it difficult;* **you** *were the one who beat yourself up, judged yourself and made it so hard on yourself. It was not necessary.*

But when we look at your life that is how you approached life. You did not approach life in joy and eagerness. You approached life as a task to be done. You were in survival most of the time. I do realize that the world was a difficult place to be in that era. But you see, up on my ship, *The New Jerusalem*, we do not have time such as you know it. We do not approach any task as being a *force of nature*. We just go to the task and know we will do it. And yes, we may change the way we approach it in mid-stream, so to speak. We give ourselves that flexibility so that any decision of ours is not set in stone.

That is the message I wish to give to you, readers, as you struggle with what you perceive is the way to ascend. There ought not to be any struggle—only flexibility; only your ability to change and take another direction. You see, I am speaking about another face of Ascension, and it is called *flexibility*. How flexible can you be?

Some people are very flexible. They can change with a click of their fingers. Other people cannot change until they are halfway through their project. They become so mired down that they say to themselves, *whoa, I don't think this is the way I am supposed to do this!* They then will turn and think of another way to approach their task.

I wish to say to you that if you are in your heart, your soul will direct you. Your soul will give you directions on how to play something out, how to make the connection. You would be surprised, readers, how many people in this world do not pay attention to their soul's guidance. And yes, some of the struggle could be what you are facing from your contract. However, there is such a thing as using what is called a *heavy hand.*

When you made up your contract with your soul and your counsel, tasks were given to you that we all, including your soul, knew you could do. There was no discussion on how you could not do it. There was only discussion about how to do it.

Maybe in a previous lifetime, you had taken a wrong turn so that the outcome was not one of joy or completion. Therefore, you took another life: *Oh, if I do it this way, then I will be able to complete this task.*

You see, before you took the next lifetime, there were long hours of planning. You met with all the players you would meet—the antagonists, the helpers, the teachers, the counselors—while in a body. You had it pretty well set up. It was a perfect plan when you left

Heaven (*I am chuckling.*), when you left my ship, I will say. *The New Jerusalem* can be Heaven to many.

Therefore, a face of Ascension is *flexibility,* and how you approach it becomes a lesson in itself—a task that you had agreed to. It may sound somewhat strange to you readers, but yes, *how to ascend* was in your game plan. You may be surprised to know that, yes, you have been working on this for more than one lifetime.

Most people will have several lifetimes to get the task done. You see, they have so much in their contract that they wish to complete that it can bring up more tasks. If they did not get them correct, it could entail more lifetimes. It takes a while to make that Ascension journey. So I have listed *flexibility* as a face. You may wonder, what is left? I will say to you, what about *emotions* such as *laughter* and *joy?* Are those not also faces of Ascension?

We in the upper Ethers, shall we say, while in our ships, work in such joy. We are laughing most the time. We can see the ridiculous in the ridiculousness. And we laugh. *Oh, is that what is going on!* If we can, and if it is our stuff, we will change. But we do not beat ourselves up for trying. That is a fallacy of humanity. It hates to be wrong. People get so caught up in what they are doing with a certain idea. If it does not pan out, they beat themselves up. They forget about being flexible.

People seem to have a fallacy that anything they attempt ought to be a perfect way of doing something. There is no flexibility worked into it. There is little joy of accomplishment, for the past was so difficult for them. They forget their humor. And, of course, I am speaking of the humor of the higher degree—never at someone—but humor with someone.

So we have *flexibility* and now *humor* as faces.

What do you think is another face? How about determination, perseverance? Do you give up when the task becomes difficult? Or do you persevere? Say you are a student at college. You have taken a course that is more difficult than expected. Do you just stop going to class and give up; quit the class and say you will take something else? Or do you find a tutor to help you; study harder and persevere until it is done?

Do you know, readers, on the different space ships that surround the world keeping it safe that many times we have found ourselves in difficult positions? We may have noted that a huge asteroid is heading for Earth. What are we going to do about it? Do we ignore it and let it happen? At the rate it is traveling, it will create quite a huge hole when it hits Earth. Or do we call a counsel, tackle the problem and decide what to do—aim our devices which emit beams of Light to break it up into smaller pieces? Or we can push the asteroid into another direction so it will not hit Earth. We have done this for far too numerous times to even count.

Humanity thinks that when there are ships around Earth, it is to take over the people, to steal their resources. There may have been times in antiquity when that was done. But no longer do you have to worry about that. We come in peace. We come in love and we come in the Christ Consciousness of the Creator.

But to get back to *perseverance,* I was telling you this because we persevered to push that asteroid(s) away from your world. Therefore, you can add *perseverance* as a face of Ascension. By the time you readers get through this book, you will have quite a list of what to do or what you have done on your journey to Ascension. It will be a glorious time for you. I will not go into it much more because I do not want to take away the surprise and the feeling of awe you will experience when it all happens for you. It is a glorious time in your life.

I thank you for having me come. I have enjoyed my time with you immensely. I am signing off now so another may speak.

Thank you so much, Ashtar; it is so nice to talk with you again. Oh, my dear one, if you only knew how your star shines in the Heavenlies. You can always reach me. I am in that ship you know, *The New Jerusalem*. Greetings, dear one.

Thank you, Ashtar; greetings to you!

5:50 AM. Well, precious one, that was short and sweet. Do you wish to bring in another one?

Yes, there is still room on the tape, and it is only ten of six.

All right, let's see who is next here. Ah, we have Djwal Khul.

Oh, what fun; good, thank you!

DJWAL KHUL

So my dear Author, we meet again. I am Djwal Khul.

Thank you, Lord, for coming and yes, I am plowing through this book on Ascension.

Well, you are doing a wonderful service again. I shall say *once again* for you have written many books, and I have been honored to partake in some of those chapters. *Yes.*

To you readers, I am also known as *The Tibetan,* and I guided Alice Bailey through her many books and met this author, Chako, along the way. So I am always delighted when I can pop in again.

The other Masters who have spoken earlier have brought to your attention different faces for Ascension. As you readers are beginning to see, there are so many paths that can be taken—so many ways to do it. Be *flexible,* as Ashtar has said. Be *humorous;* be in *joy;* have *perseverance.* And I am not sure there is more to say.

I wrote about *Initiations* for Alice Bailey; the different *Rays* that were involved. Now a days we do not speak that much about the Rays and Initiations. Certainly Initiations are involved. In my books we used to count them. The first one meant this; the second one meant that. The fourth one was call *The Crucifixion.* But you have grown beyond that. You are up in the double digits, your magnificent achievements.

What Ray do you think you use on your way to Ascension? I will tell you that eventually you use all of them, but then one becomes dominant. And it is the *Love* one—*Christ Force Energy.* Some people are put off by that term, the *Christ Force.* It throws them back into their religion or the fact they had no religion. But dear souls, it is **not** a religion. It is an energy, and yes, it was brought to Earth by the Christ. But that is just a name. You have had many great men pass through

49

history. Look at Einstein and his *Law of Relativity* that he awakened humanity to. Christ brought in the *Christ Consciousness*. Give the man credit! And I am chuckling. We are speaking, dear souls, of the energy that you carry.

Some people have what we call *shallow hearts*. They find it difficult to love very deeply. Then that is attached to how well they receive.

You know there is an old song the people in the Southern regions of America sang and maybe still do—*Them Bones*. The lyrics tell how each bone is connected to the next bone, and it is sung in a sing-song way. *YouTube* has different renditions, but we enjoyed the dancing skeletons. At the end, the narrator identifies the bones and gives their definitions and purposes. The song then can become a learning tool for anyone. It is all true and cleverly orchestrated. (*Go to YouTube and click on Bob Barner for the story-line dance of the skeletons and the music and vocals by Raul Malo et al.*)

That is what Ascension is about—*Connection*. Love connects you. Ashtar was talking about the faces and how love connects you to your heart-mind. That leads you to connect with your humor and it goes on and on. In this era, people think about Ascension, going up Jacob's ladder, or however you wish to visualize it along the way—the Initiations you go through and the different Rays that you use—the love connection, the Christ Force Energy. And if your composition is rich and knowing, then there is kindness and caring. Therefore, are you beginning to see how all is connected—how all is another face for Ascension?

While Ascension is a private affair, we will say—for only you can ascend—you cannot do it for another. You cannot take someone with you or carry someone on your coattails. However, at the same time, it is connection in all possible ways. Connection with people is not done in isolation. No longer do you go into a cave and stay there all by yourself until you ascend; or go sit under a Bodhi tree until you are enlightened.

You see, we are speaking of energies. Just as you change with flexibility, so do energies. Energies do not stay the same. They are not constant. They are changing. They are flexible. Even the love energy has changed. You may wonder how that can be. It has grown more deeply. The color is more pure.

When you are born and leave your mother's womb, you have that memory…

It was at this point that the tape ran out. I leave it up to you, dear readers, to fill in the blanks. Go within and you will connect with that memory of pure love.

7

MOTHER EARTH-GAIA

5:10 AM Friday, December 16, 2016 *Hello, precious one; we are all set to start Chapter 7. We are going to go deeper and bring forth the voice of this Mother Planet, Gaia.* Oh, what a privilege. *I will step aside now and let her speak.* Thank you.

Hello, my dear Being; I am known as Gaia, and you are a soul of my heart. It always pleases me so when I can speak with a Being such as yourself that truly loves me—that truly wants to walk upon my shores, and at the same time prepare herself to ascend. That is such joy, because that is exactly what I am doing—ascending. So we will do this together. *Yes, and thank you so much for giving me your time.* It is my deepest pleasure.

Now, the theme of this book so far seems to be the *Faces of Ascension*. What a clever idea. The Beings, the Souls, work so hard to help the people along the way. While I see, of course, what they are doing— nothing much gets by me, I must admit—still, it is gratifying to witness another one's dedication, for I, too, am dedicated to going forward with this, forever reaching upward.

So let me see if I can describe another face that has not been mentioned. I know that *joy* and *humor* and *perseverance* have been spoken about. But what about playfulness, playing along my shores when the ocean waters are breaking, *laughing* and in such joy? I would, therefore, like to add the *face of laughter*. Souls are so dedicated to their task that at times they forget. When they are playful and laughing, that too is ascending—going up that ladder, racing up that ladder, playfully poking each other with much laughter.

Laughter cleans the decks, shall we say. If a person is in a bad mood and someone or something brings out mirth in that person, the dark mood disappears. The vibration rises. So you see, laughter becomes a useful tool to help you along the way.

Many people are grieving as loved ones, friends, have transitioned to the Heavenlies. We want to shout to them *read Chako's books on Transitions,* for they are just trading places, shall we say. Their work was done here on my shores, and now they are joyous and having a wonderful time most likely in the Heavenlies.

And yes, even as the tears roll down their cheeks, they can laugh, remembering the good times they had with their friends. So by all means, raise your vibrations by using laughter. The Irish are correct when they hold their wakes and people, perhaps, imbibe a little too much in the good drink. But they laugh uproariously and slap each other on their backs. The soul who was passing was there among them, sharing in the stories relating to him or her.

It is the right approach, for it is a time for rejoicing and raising one's vibration, as one goes upward and climbing. The *laughter* and *wakes* and even *grieving* are all part of ascending. When one says *how can grieving be a part of ascending*, I say *it involves saying goodbye and wishing someone great happiness as that person transitions;* or if it is you personally, you are letting go. Ah, did I just name another face—*letting go?*

If you were on a balloon ride, you would have to let go; you cannot hold on to any of the ropes that tether the balloon. By letting go of the ropes/cords, it allows the balloon to float up into the sky. As you ascend, you must let go. What is holding you back? But you see, you may not realize that you are being held back. You are only trying to save or hang on to something or someone who is dear to your heart.

You do not realize that by letting go, you will then journey in a different direction. You will have a different experience from what you let go of. Many times for people it is a possessive love. They have the hardest time letting go of that person, place, or thing—that definition of a noun.

So, the faces we have so far are *laughter* and *letting go*. You may be wondering how I as a planet can be experiencing those two faces so that I may ascend. But I am speaking of the many people who are on my shores. I hear laughter and they may be dancing. I see people letting go, and therefore, I can let go. And yes, I know that many times in my letting go, it creates tossing of the ground and waters—earthquakes and tsunamis are all part of my letting go. I do not wish to possess you either. This is my body that I have offered you. I have offered you this place where you can experience the different dramas you have set up for your life. When people fall into their dark sides, it all depends on how long they are going to stay here.

I use fire many times—a fire that rages through the forests and hamlets. It is cleansing, cleansing out the dead wood, the dark energies. It can be frightening because it is so powerful. But bear in mind, all who die in those flames are honoring their contract. They wrote that up before they were born. And as their life progressed, each step brought them closer to where that fire would help them ascend— help them transition. So can we add *fire* as a face for Ascension?

You have been told there are many, many ways to ascend. So why wouldn't fire be a face? Of course it is—a cleansing, a purification. As the different Masters have come in and expressed their views on the *Faces of Ascension*, I hope it has become clear to you readers that it is not necessary to use **all** the faces. I am sure there are many of you not too happy to read about the *fire face*. But that was in your contract; or is in your contract—death by fire.

You readers may be wondering, what about all the wars—bombs are dropped; bodies are blown up; airplanes are shot down? Is there a face in all of that turmoil? There is a face, but it is not one that helps a person to ascend, per se. It is one that helps a person to transition. And **if** that transition is part of one's ascension—perhaps in war—then one can say that war can be a face of Ascension. But I will say that that would be a negative approach, and I would not recommend it. *Peace* and *Love* would be a better way. So is *Peace* a face of Ascension? It most certainly is.

We call this time of year the *Holidays*—for the Jewish population it is *Hanukah*, for others it is *Christmas*. There can be a frenzy of gift buying for people who are in good will. They are joyous and laughing; they are giving and long for Peace. Did I just describe another face—*giving*? People who live on my planet give to me all the time. They nurture my flowers and trees; they feed the animals that roam or fly through the forests. They give to others which helps everyone raise his or her vibration. Remember in the previous chapter where it spoke of the shallow heart? It is in the giving that allows that heart to grow, which, of course, raises your vibration. One could make a statement that every positive act that you do is a step up Jacob's ladder—a step up to Ascension.

You see, dear readers, how Ascension can mean different things to different people—your outlook on life. Is it positive or pessimistic in that the worst is going to happen? There are people who always think the worst will happen. And there are others who start out thinking everything will be wonderful and then are shocked when they find they have hit that part of their life that is contract and their world comes crashing down around them. How will they handle all of that—to be pessimistic and let it absorb them? Or do they know that if they make a change in how they are perceiving something, it will bring to them positive effects.

For me, when the wars have stopped in a certain segment of me, it is a relief to have the chaos stopped, the hurting of people stopped, to have the blowing up of artifacts stopped. I then have to bring cleansing to those areas. I may cause a tsunami to wash ashore to cleanse it and give the people an opportunity to finish their contract or to move on.

You see, I am Gaia, your mother. And like your human mother who cleans up after you have spilt your milk or whatever else you may do, I as Gaia, also have to clean up after your messes so the green grass can grow again and the trees can stretch to new heights and the flowers can bloom again. Peace can reign again; laughter can spring forth from the children instead of tears. All of this then allows me to raise my vibrations and to ascend into the next higher dimension.

Many people do not think of a planet acting out as their mother. I am also known as the *school house* in the sky. Souls can learn a variety of lessons. But the time has come where I, too, need to ascend. I cannot let humanity's folly stop me. Just as children finish school and go forward with their life's purposes, I, too, have my purpose. I, too, am important in the scheme of things. I, too, wish for peace and to hear joy and laughter; mostly, I, too, need love. And *love,* of course, is a face of Ascension.

Dear author, thank you for being one of my spokespersons. Thank you for my opportunity to talk to the readers. This may be a new concept for some that the planet they are living on is a living organism with a heart—breathing, just like you do—loving, just like all of you love, for which I am most grateful.

I greet you now; I AM Gaia.

Thank you so much, Gaia. It truly was lovely.

You are most welcome, dear soul.

All right, my precious one—another chapter in the can, I think is the expression. You did it.

Yes, yes, I did; thank you (*long sigh of relief*).

Until we meet again; I AM Jeshua.

Thank you, Jeshua. 5:55 AM.

8

KUTHUMI

5:55 AM Friday, January 6, 2017.

Hello, precious one; you are all set to bring in Chapter 8. The book is progressing very nicely and we are most pleased. We will be bringing forth another Master who has channeled Chapters for your other books before, so I will step back and let him introduce himself. Thank you, Jeshua.

Good morning, my dear one, I am known as Kuthumi.

Oh, Kuthumi, it has been so long since I last talked with you. (I check his energy with my pendulum to make sure he is who he says he is and not a figment of my imagination.)

We Masters who are lined up for your book are very pleased, for of course, Ascension is a subject that needs an explanation to the majority of people. You are finding out, I am sure, that Ascension has many faces. I will be bringing you even more faces that you and the readers may not have thought of.

I always like to start *In the beginning...* so I will start off and say in the beginning when the world was so dense and the dimensions were not very high, people did not think of *Ascension*. They only thought, perhaps, of where they were going to get their next meal. It was always a question of *do I need to go hunt or is there a war to fight? Live or die* was their limited motto.

Then as humanity evolved, it found it had choices—whether to go hunt for a meal or to relax by a brook or go courting the women, for they were a robust, earthy bunch.

As soon as their inner philosophy started wondering what was beyond death, then they were ready to think whether they needed to prepare themselves to advance, to raise their energy vibrations. You see, it had not been all that long ago when people had even thought about personal vibrations.

They then just went a little beyond the *live or die* mentality and started wondering whether it made a difference on how they lived their life. Humanity was so used to just surviving. But now with choices, they saw that perhaps those who gave were more apt to receive. As we look at it during this era of 2017, which was unheard of back in antiquity, people of a more evolved consciousness knew that one needed to *give and receive.* In so doing, it automatically raised one's vibrations. Therefore, you can see that that becomes a face of Ascension, can you not?

Yes, and as you have said, I had not thought of that as being a face of Ascension.

So, we will say that *giving and receiving* is definitely a face of Ascension, for it raises your vibration level. Of course, the more your vibration is raised, the more Light your body can receive. Consequently, there is another face to Ascension. *What is your Light quotient?* One does not hear that question very often among humanity now, but the more Light a soul carries, the higher becomes its vibration and he or she or it has climbed another step or two up Jacob's ladder. We could almost start calling it the *Ascension Ladder.* So we have *giving and receiving* and one's *Light quotient* as faces so far.

You may wonder whether we have run through all of the faces. I will say to you and the readers that the faces of Ascension are almost uncountable, for you are looking at and counting personalities of the soul. Each personality, of course, carries its own vibration. The higher the vibration, the more Light, for one is more able to receive. Therefore, *vibration* is also a face.

As humanity traverses this new year of 2017, it will find it trying at times to keep a balance. There is so much going on in the political arena in America that it is difficult for people to stay balanced, to not judge, to let go and let God. Not everyone, of course, agrees with who was elected President, but that is the way of life.

It would be a dull world indeed if there were only one way of thinking, for through adversity are born new ideas—a spice that feeds and perhaps wakes up people so that they start thinking on their own. Therefore, if there are enough people opposed to a certain idea, then there can be change. And, of course, *change* is a face of Ascension.

Adversity can be a face, but it is more of a catalyst. I believe it was Gaia in the previous chapter who said that war can change one's way of thinking but she did not recommend it for Ascension. Adversity then can be used as a catalyst. Of course, one does not usually decide consciously *I will create adversity in order to change people's minds.* It is already in one's DNA.

Psychologists call the action *passive aggressive.* Are you a passive type or are you aggressive? That often becomes paired in marriage. This author once heard a woman exclaim, *I hate passive husbands.* And, of course, her personality was well known as being aggressive. She was a do-er. So you see, dear friends, I have added a few more faces for you.

When authors write fiction books, they take on different ways of being. They become their characters. Perhaps the most famous characters are Rhett Butler and Scarlet O'Hara in *Gone with the Wind* by Margaret Mitchell. It is a beautiful book about love and adversities during the war between the states of America.

You see, President Lincoln had the spiritual contract to lead America out of slavery. He knew he would be assassinated over this, but a change had to come about, for it is not healthy for a country and its people to be so divided. That is why Democratic countries hold elections and vote in a leader. If that leader does not lead honestly and with integrity, he or she can be impeached and ousted. Then a new leader with a different personality can take over. A President needs to have an aggressive personality. He cannot lead well if he is a passive type.

General Eisenhower is a good example. America voted in a retired general—Dwight Eisenhower—to lead them in the post-world war era. Therefore, the *personality* can be a face of Ascension. If you were passive in one lifetime, you will be aggressive in the next when the soul is always seeking *balance*—another face of Ascension.

There must be balance in your life. You look at scales and you watch how the numbers (*or arms*) can go up or down, showing the physical weight of something; or if musing—you could ask yourself *how much do I love? How much do I give? How much do I receive? How much is this ambition or aggression? How much is in adversity? What is the balance?* I have touched on just a few more ideas for you readers on the importance for balance in your lives—the importance of love, for you will find that *love* is a great balancer.

In my youth, I was what one might call *head-strong*. My mind was turning out ideas faster than one could play them out. I was a *thinker* and what one would call now, a *philosopher* in my own way. I enjoyed reading, and I would pick up many ideas by reading the philosophies of those who lived before me. Then I started teaching, and it gave me great joy to see the students' minds blossom and develop.

When I could see a student who was developing rapidly, I overshadowed him or her. (It is called being *overlighted* now.) When the person spoke, I was speaking. This was a great satisfaction for both of us, for I could still lead the person. The student was developing the higher centers in the body, bringing different dimensions to the body.

Therefore, that also became a way of Ascension, for those people who had developed their physical vessels enough so that a master with a slight adjustment of his or her energy could overlight a fellow student. We are all students. We were partners to bring new ideas and advance humanity's thinking.

I can say that with this author, I have come to her, but Jeshua was the one who pointed me in her direction. She and I had made the connection many years ago in her other books when Jeshua brought us together. Therefore, dear readers, it is a face of Ascension to have the help and the energy connection with a higher vibration. It is like being lifted up.

To think in infantile terms, a toddler is lifted up by its mother or father. The toddler grows up with the parents guiding the adult child. When the young adult keeps maturing and developing its vibrations, a connection can be made with a higher entity. In this case, it was Jeshua. You could say he is still lifting up humanity. Having a *higher energy connection* is also a face of Ascension. Of course, not everyone makes that connection consciously, but it is there.

I have come to the end of my time with all of you, and I so appreciate this opportunity for me. It has been most delightful. I will step aside now for another. Greetings.

Thank you, Lord, thank you. You have given us all several faces we had not even thought of before.

You are most welcome, dear one, greetings.

All right, dear one; that was our Kuthumi!

Oh my, this just keeps going on and on doesn't?

Yes, dear one, yes; but the book is gradually coming to its end. We, too, are most appreciative. Until next time, I AM Jeshua.

Thank you, Jeshua. 6:40 AM.

9

GOD

01-13-17 Friday, 5:30 AM.

Good morning dear one; you are all set to bring in Chapter 9. This entity you will bring forth you have channeled several times. He is always delighted to come forth. I will step aside now and let this beautiful Being speak.

Good morning my precious child of my heart. I am God, your Father.

Oh Lord, you come to me before I can write the Epic that you asked of me. (God calls Chapters, Epics.)

Yes, it seems so. There is a little bit more time before the Epic I asked of you/Jeshua to write is needed. But this morning it is all about the *Faces of Ascension.*

I, as a Luminescent, see humanity in droves moving toward Ascension. I see their struggles with their contracts. They set their game plans and then find sometimes that they have bit off more than they can chew. There are windows of opportunity that we described in previous books where the soul can just pull the plug and end that lifetime. Many are doing that. Whereas if they had stayed steadfast and addressed the problems they were having with a certain task on their journey, they would find that they could have overcome that, be the winner, and advance their vibrations even more.

The Creator is very aware with what humanity is up to. It looks at first glance that people are not advancing because of all the killing that is going on. But if you will look at the deeper picture, you will see that the dark is rising up and out. People are shooting police officers right and left it looks like—showing their true colors. Many times their hearts have been torn and they are seeking love, but they go into rage and/or mental illness, then their heart shrinks even more.

It is at that point that they need guidance—a loving word or a loving hand to hold. But they are so broken that they cannot always accept what is right there for them to receive. When an entity becomes that broken, it is better that he/she dies so that the soul can be healed. *(There are times when the person has been killed by the police or the state Justice system.)*

If the soul is that broken when he/she dies, my Angels are instructed to just put the soul back into total essence. It is then disintegrated. It is similar to when a child blows soap bubbles. He or she puts her finger into the bubble and it will pop and disintegrate into many pieces and is then gone. You can use this mental picture, readers, of what it may look like when a soul is put back into total essence.

You might be wondering readers when I speak of the *faces*, for so many have been described in the previous chapters. In order to clarify and make it easier to understand the process, I will tell you that every thought, deed, and action will have a featured face of Ascension. As you read this book, many thoughts and questions will arise for you readers. You will start going through the previous line of thought that you have had, perhaps. Or you will start going through the different acts that you have done and categorizing them.

Were they of a positive nature—of the Light? If you can say *yes* and replicate them as such, then they will become steps up the ascension ladder. If not, then reframe the thought and if possible, the deed so that it will become the face of Ascension. Therefore, *reframing, retraining* are faces. To simplify this, any time you can change a negative into a positive, that act becomes a face of Ascension.

The wonderful thing about this is rarely is it too late to act upon this deed to restore it to Light. Of course if you have shot someone dead, you will not be able to change that act. I am speaking of what can be acts of kindness. Maybe you did not smile at someone who would have sent you a returning smile. Perhaps you did not help someone in the grocery store to lift something off a shelf that she could not reach. Think of your acts.

Think of your acts toward animals. Any act of cruelty is certainly not an act for Ascension. However, *hugging* the animal so it can feel your love becomes a face of Ascension.

To simplify, I am speaking in terms of good (*Light*) and not good (*dark*) deeds, for those of the Light become faces of Ascension.

In America, it is a transition period when a newly elected President will soon take office. As people demonstrate in different ways their approval, or demonstrate their disapproval, one quickly can see the depth of their heart.

Yesterday, January 12, 2017, President Barack Obama bestowed the *Presidential Medal of Freedom*, the highest award that a President can give, to Vice-President Joe Biden. The kindness and the love was palpable between the President and the Vice-President. Those who were watching on TV, as this author was, saw the Vice-President's emotions—or one could say, saw his heart.

He has had what one could call a rough journey with loved ones dying. There is a saying, *he wore his heart on his sleeve.* One could see how deeply that man loves. With all the trauma of family members dying, his heart has grown. He talked of how he had to lean on his sons when his wife and child had died in a car accident. Then he had to lean on his second wife when his son, Bo was dying of a severe illness. He almost sold his home in order to pay for the medical expenses. But President Obama urged him not to, saying he would pay the bills. He freely spoke of those times of needing someone to lean on. He was not ashamed to talk about it. He was able to reach out and receive.

I am speaking about the hearts of people. Having a shallow heart verses a deep heart, which one do you think brings you higher vibrations and the higher dimensions of Ascension? So there is another face, is it not? A *deep heart,* a large heart is a face of Ascension. And Vice-President Biden was able to *receive* which has already been noted as a face of Ascension.

I have spoken about several different aspects so that you will get the picture that Ascension—or the faces of Ascension—are many and different. If you talk to those on the other side who have ascended at a high level and compare notes, you will find that each got to where he or she is by using different faces. As the Lord Kuthumi said, the faces of Ascension are uncountable.

Dear readers, you are just starting the year of 2017. It is the year of *love*, giving out love, receiving love. But love is also a catalyst; do you not see? It cannot stand beside darkness, for it is Light. Light and love are synonymous. The more love that you bring to you and the deeper your heart becomes it flushes out that which is not of high vibration. Dark thoughts, mean thoughts, and those thoughts of revenge; the lower emotions of anger, rage, anxiety, worry, fear, all of that rises to the top. Love displaces all of that which raises your vibration.

Therefore, dear ones, I watch over you; I know you; I see you. You cannot hide from me and I love you. Please take in what I have said. There is much to learn in my words.

Dear author, I step aside now. I eagerly look forward to the *epic* (which I prefer calling a chapter) that you and Jeshua will write for my God book.

Love to all of you; I am God, the Luminescence of this world.

Oh thank you Lord; thank you so much.

You are most welcome. Greetings. 6:25 AM.

All right dear one; you brought in another chapter.

Yes, God presented some different ways to look at the faces of Ascension.

Yes; we will be wrapping up this book very shortly now. So until next time, Greetings.

Thank you Jeshua.

CONCLUSION SANANDA

01-19-2017 Thursday, 5:25 AM.

Good morning, precious one; I am Jeshua. Archangel Michael has brought down a pillar of Light protection and put it around you. Therefore, you are all set. You, on a higher level, and I and other Masters had a discussion as to whether we wished to end the book and this would be the Conclusion, *or to bring forth a few more Masters and have a few more Chapters.*

It was decided that we would conclude this book because the Masters have given the readers a good working idea of the Ascension process. Therefore, it will be Sananda who will give the Conclusion *to this book.* OK.

Dear readers, many Masters have come forth to give you little tidbits as to how Ascension works—what it is. As you have read these chapters—and I hope you have and not jumped to the last chapter in the book as is the habit of many of you *(chuckles)*—you will see that almost everything that you do, as our Luminescent has just told you, is an aspect of Ascension.

The smallest act of a smile, or giving and receiving, just living in as positive a way that you know how is a step up the Ascension ladder. When Ascension is presented as a **natural process** for the soul to raise its vibrations, that then **is** Ascension. So much has been spoken in books and on the Internet about Ascension that it has been made out to be a somewhat nebulous goal that is unattainable for the average person, and that is not true. Every thought and deed is a gradual incline to Ascension.

In this book, many Masters have eagerly given their thoughts as well as their time on Ascension. Each one presented a different aspect. It gave you readers a perspective that perhaps you had not thought of. It brought Ascension down to Earth—grounded it—so you can see it is quite the goal that everyone can strive for.

At the end of this journey, there may be several more to take. All will ascend if their heart and soul are in the Light. There is no ending to this; it is open-ended. Many of you may think that once we Masters have made that august body of scholars and philosophers and have received our Mastership, that that is it. We have ascended, and that's it. Nothing could be further from the truth.

We, too, are constantly striving to improve ourselves, to learn, to raise our vibration, to enter an even higher dimension. While we do not have that constantly in the forefront of our everyday lives, we do know that everything that we do either adds or subtracts to our energies and vibrations.

And just like humanity, or maybe I ought not to put it like that, we, too, make mistakes. If there is a certain task that we take on, we may find that we have to rethink that. We may have to change directions, for what we had been doing was not solving the problem. We then had to think of another way of getting the job done. However, the difference, you see, between us Masters and humanity is we do not give up! We keep persevering. Maybe that is the most difficult lesson humanity has to learn—persevere and get the act accomplished.

There were times when this author kind of groaned inwardly, *oh, I've got to get up early,* for when one channels at an early hour, the energies in the ethers are less congested—clearer—so that the channeling is more pure. Therefore, she awakens early, a few minutes before 5:00 AM and sits and channels. You see—she perseveres. This is her 15th book. How do you think you she got that many done? She persevered; she never gave up. She may have slowed down, taking more time between chapters. But it was not in her reality to just toss everything aside, including me, who helps channel her books. Therefore, dear readers, I suggest that *perseverance* is one of the main acts toward Ascension.

I really do not have that much more to say. The various Masters have done their thing and are now off doing other acts. We do hope this book has provided you some insight as to what Ascension is. It is not nebulous. It is everything ou do, whether it is an upward or downward journey. As I have said, if there are fits and starts on your journey, you can always take another lifetime to finish your journey.

I bid you farewell, dear readers, and I bless you on your journey. I AM Sananda, the Christ of this Universe. Greetings.

Oh thank you, Lord. It is kind of a relief (chuckles) to have finished this book.

Yes, I can see that. And you still have the organization of it to do and all the other little sections you still have to write (*Foreword, Acknowledgments, etc.*).

I thank you, Masters, for all that you did for me for this book. You didn't have to come (chuckles)! You didn't have to come and give so graciously of yourself. I am so appreciative.

All right, dear one, you have a great deal to do yet. And tomorrow is the Inauguration (01-20-2017). Enjoy watching all the festivities. It will be a grand day.

Until we meet again, precious one, I AM Jeshua/ Sananda.

Thank you, Lord.

And I also want to thank Arch Angel Michael who so graciously made sure I was protected by his pillar of Light.

5:50 AM

EPILOGUE

02-31-17 Yay, I did it! My fifteenth book is finished—the channeling part, that is. Now there is just a bit to write—the *EPILOGUE,* for example.

Readers, did you notice the change in what first was going to be the title of the book? (*The **Truth** of Ascension.*) Each Master who gave us a teaching on Ascension talked mainly of *The **Faces** of Ascension.* When I finally saw the direction in which the book was headed, I changed the noun in the title from *Truth* to *Faces.* And, of course, there is truth in what they say, but they describe their lesson in a way I had never thought of by using the noun *Face(s).*

So, dear readers, this is it for now. I am back in the space of *letting go; letting God.* I am clueless as to what is next!

Until we meet again, I AM Chako. Blessings.

I do not participate in social media, but I am open to hearing from you any time at azchako@aol.com.

My books are available at **Trafford 888-232-4444** or on **Amazon. com.**

I thank Archangel Michael for his protection while I am channeling. Knowing that his pillar of Light and hundreds of Angels are surrounding me sustains me and allows me the freedom to proceed.

I so appreciate your help, Jeshua, in bringing forth the various Presenters for our book. My love and thanks to you.

Hugs, Chako.

READER'S NOTES

ABOUT THE AUTHOR

Verling (CHAKO) Priest, PhD was born in Juneau, Alaska, hence her name of Cheechako, shortened to just Chako by her mother, a medical doctor, and her father, an Orthodontist. Chako was raised in Napa, CA. She attended the University of California at Berkeley where she met her future husband. Upon their marriage and after his training as a Navy pilot, they settled into the military way of life. They lived twelve years outside of the United States Mainland in various places, which included Hawaii, Viet Nam, Australia, and Greece. Little did she know that these exotic lands and peoples were preparing her for her spiritual awakening years hence?

After her husband's retirement from the Navy, they resettled in Napa, California. It was during this time that she returned to school at Berkeley, transferred to Sonoma University where she earned her first two degrees in Psychology. Chako then entered the doctoral program at the Institute of Transpersonal Psychology (ITP), renamed Sufi

University, which is now located in Palo Alto, CA. She successfully completed that program which consisted of a Master, as well as the Doctorate in Transpersonal Psychology. Ten years and four degrees later she was able to pursue her passion for Metaphysical and New Age Thought—her introduction into the realm of the Spiritual Hierarchy and the Ascended Lords and Masters.

In 1988, Dr. Priest moved to Minnetonka, Minnesota. She co-authored a program called, *Second Time Around* for those with recurring cancer for Methodist Hospital. She, as a volunteer, also facilitated a grief group for Pathways of Minneapolis, and had a private practice.

She studied with a spiritual group in Minnetonka led by Donna Taylor and the Teacher, a group of 5 highly developed entities trance-channeled by Donna. The group traveled extensively all over the world working with the energy grids of the planet and regaining parts of their energies that were still in sacred areas waiting to be reclaimed by them, the owners. They climbed in and out of the pyramids in Egypt, tromped through the Amazon forest in Venezuela, rode camels at Sinai, and climbed the Mountain. Hiked the paths at Qumran, trod the ancient roadways in Petra, Jordan, and walked where the Master Yeshua/Jesus walked in Israel.

The time came, November 1999, when Chako was guided to move to Arizona—her next period of growth. This is where she found her beloved Masters, who in reality had always been with her. They were **all** ready for her next phase, bringing into the physical many books—mind-provoking books, telepathically received by her, from these highly evolved, beautiful, loving Beings. Each book stretches her capabilities, as well as her belief systems. Nevertheless, it is a challenge she gladly embraces.

It is now February, 2017. She has finished writing her fifteenth book, *THE FACES OF ASCENSION.* Blessings!

Comments to azchako@aol.com

Godumentary.com/chako

LIST OF PREVIOUS BOOKS

Verling CHAKO Priest, Ph.D.

The Ultimate Experience, the Many Paths to God series:

BOOKS 1, 2, & 3 REVISITED (2011)

ISBN # 978-1-4269-7664-3 (sc)

ISBN# 978-1-4269-7665-0 (e-book)

REALITIES of the CRUCIFIXION (2006)

ISBN # 1-978-4669-2148-1

MESSAGES from the HEAVENLY HOSTS (2007)

ISBN # 1-4251-2550-6

YOUR SPACE BROTHERS and SISTERS GREET YOU! (2008) ISBN # 978-1-4251-6302-0

TEACHINGS of the MASTERS of LIGHT (2008)

ISBN # 978-1-4251-8573-2

PAULUS of TARSUS (2010)

ISBN # 978-1-4669-209-1 (sc)

ISBN # 978-1-4669-2090-3 (e-book)

THE GODDESS RETURNS to EARTH (2010)

ISBN # 978-1-4269-3563-3

ISBN # 978-1-4269-3564-0 (e-book)

JESUS: MY BELOVED CONNECTION TO

HUMANITY AND THE SEA Revised Edition (2013)

CO-AUTHOR REV. CYNTHIA WILLIAMS

ISBN # 978-1-4669-7641-2(sc)

ISBN # 978-1-4669-7642-9(hc)

ISBN # 978-1-4669-7640-5(e)

MASTERS' TALES of NOW (2013)

ISBN #978-1-4907-1351-9 (sc)

ISBN #978-4907-1350-2 (hc)

ISBN #978-1-4907-1352-6 (e-book)

RELATIONSHIPS (2014)

ISBN #978-1-4907-5188-7 (sc)

#978 1 4907-5190-0 (hc)

#978-1-4907-5189-4 (e)

TRANSITIONS (2015)

ISBN # 978-1-4907-5836—7 (sc)

#978-1-4907-5838-1 (hc)

#978-1-4907-5837-4 (e)

TRANSITIONS II (2015)

ISBN #978-1-4907-6794-9 (sc)

#978-1-4907-6796-3 (hc)

#978-1-4907-6795-6 (e)

THE FACES OF ASCENSION (2017)

ISBN #978-1-4907-8112-9 (sc)

ISBN #978-1-4907-8113-6 (hc)

ISBN #978-1-4907-8114-3 (e)

Available at Trafford: 1-888-232-4444

Or, Amazon.com

www.godumentary.com/chako.

Printed in the United States
By Bookmasters